W9-ADW-832

THOMAS CRANE PUBLIC LIBRARY
QUINCY MA

CITY APPROPRIATION

New York

Niels R. Jensen

Visit us at
www.abdopublishing.com

Published by ABDO Publishing Company, 8000 West 78th Street, Suite 310, Edina, Minnesota 55439 USA. Copyright ©2010 by Abdo Consulting Group, Inc. International copyrights reserved in all countries. No part of this book may be reproduced in any form without written permission from the publisher. The Checkerboard Library™ is a trademark and logo of ABDO Publishing Company.

Printed in the United States.

Editor: John Hamilton
Graphic Design: Sue Hamilton
Cover Illustration: Neil Klinepier
Cover Photo: iStock Photo

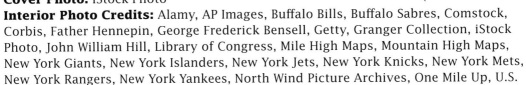

Manufactured with paper containing at least 10% post-consumer waste

Interior Photo Credits: Alamy, AP Images, Buffalo Bills, Buffalo Sabres, Comstock, Corbis, Father Hennepin, George Frederick Bensell, Getty, Granger Collection, iStock Photo, John William Hill, Library of Congress, Mile High Maps, Mountain High Maps, New York Giants, New York Islanders, New York Jets, New York Knicks, New York Mets, New York Rangers, New York Yankees, North Wind Picture Archives, One Mile Up, U.S. Navy, and the U.S. State Department.

Statistics: State population statistics taken from 2008 U.S. Census Bureau estimates. City and town population statistics taken from July 1, 2007, U.S. Census Bureau estimates. Land and water area statistics taken from 2000 Census, U.S. Census Bureau.

Library of Congress Cataloging-in-Publication Data

Jensen, Niels R., 1949-
  New York / Niels R. Jensen.
      p. cm. -- (The United States)
  Includes index.
  ISBN 978-1-60453-667-6
  1. New York (State)--Juvenile literature. I. Title.

F119.3.J46 2009
974.7--dc22
                                2008052318

Table of Contents

The Empire State 4

Quick Facts 6

Geography 8

Climate and Weather 12

Plants and Animals 14

History 18

Did You Know? 24

People 26

Cities 30

Transportation 34

Natural Resources 36

Industry 38

Sports 40

Entertainment 42

Timeline 44

Glossary 46

Index 48

The Empire State

New York is one of the most populous and important states in the country. New York's vast wealth and natural resources earned it the nickname "The Empire State."

New York has attracted many new immigrants to the United States. Forty percent of Americans have at least one ancestor who first came through the state. The Statue of Liberty stands on Liberty Island in New York Harbor. It is a symbol of freedom for millions of immigrants who come to America.

New York is often called "New York state." This helps people tell it apart from New York City, the nation's most populous metropolitan area. It is a powerful center for trade, banking, finance, industry, and shipping. There's always something exciting going on in New York City.

The Statue of Liberty stands
in busy New York Harbor.

Quick Facts

Name: New York was named to honor James, the Duke of York and Albany. He later became King James II of England.

State Capital: Albany, population 94,172

Date of Statehood: July 26, 1788 (11th state)

Population: 19,490,297 (3rd-most populous state)

Area (Total Land and Water): 54,556 square miles (141,299 sq km), 27th-largest state

Largest City: New York City, population 8,274,527

Nickname: The Empire State

Motto: *Excelsior* (Ever Upward)

State Bird: Bluebird

State Flower: Rose

State Gem: Garnet

State Tree: Sugar Maple

State Song: "I Love New York"

Highest Point: 5,344 feet (1,629 m), Mount Marcy

Lowest Point: 0 feet (0 m), Atlantic Ocean

Average July Temperature: 70°F (21°C)

Record High Temperature: 108°F (42°C) at Troy, July 22, 1926

Martin Van Buren

Average January Temperature: 22°F (-6°C)

Record Low Temperature: -52°F (-47°C) at Old Forge, February 18, 1979

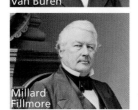

Average Annual Precipitation: 39 inches (99 cm)

Number of U.S. Senators: 2

Millard Fillmore

Number of U.S. Representatives: 29

U.S. Presidents Born in NY: Martin Van Buren, (1782-1862), Millard Fillmore (1800-1874), Theodore Roosevelt (1858-1919), and Franklin Roosevelt (1882-1945)

Theodore Roosevelt

U.S. Postal Service Abbreviation: NY

Franklin Roosevelt

QUICK FACTS

 7

Geography

The last ice age covered New York. The one-mile (1.6 km) -thick ice shield scraped the land. When it melted about 13,000 years ago, it left moraines and shaped the state's rivers, valleys, and lakes.

The Appalachian Mountains reach into New York. The Allegheny Plateau is in the western and central part of the state. The Adirondack, Catskill, Shawangunk, and Taconic Mountains are in the east. The highest point in New York is Mount Marcy. Its altitude is 5,344 feet (1,629 m) above sea level. Mount Marcy is in the scenic High Peaks region of the Adirondack Mountains. It is a popular hiking destination.

Forests cover about 62 percent of New York. Adirondack Park is a six-million-acre (2.4-million-ha) nature preserve. It is the largest of its kind outside Alaska.

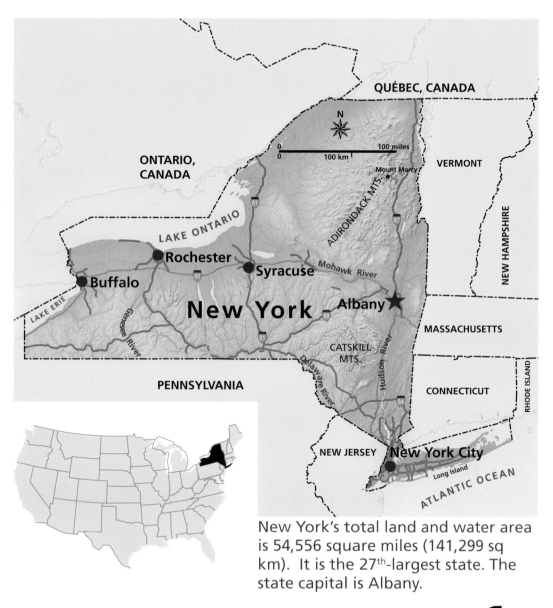

New York's total land and water area is 54,556 square miles (141,299 sq km). It is the 27th-largest state. The state capital is Albany.

New York has about 70,000 miles (112,654 km) of rivers and streams. It also includes about 4,000 lakes and ponds, and 2.4 million acres (1 million ha) of wetlands. Important rivers include the Allegheny, Delaware, Hudson, Genesee, Mohawk, and Susquehanna. The Niagara River connects Lake Erie and Lake Ontario. It also includes spectacular Niagara Falls.

Niagara Falls sits between the Canadian province of Ontario and New York state. The water flows from Lake Erie, toward Lake Ontario

Besides Lake Erie and Lake Ontario, the state's larger lakes include Lake Champlain, Lake George, and Oneida Lake. The Finger Lakes region is a fertile farming area.

The southern part of New York borders the Atlantic Ocean. Rivers and streams flow into the sea at New York City and Long Island. Long Island Sound is actually a drowned

The beautiful Watkins Glen State Park is part of the Finger Lakes region.

valley that was long ago carved by the glaciers. Today, the island has moraines and good farmland.

Climate and Weather

Weather in New York changes a lot. There can be large swings in temperature. There are four seasons,

Summer heat waves often strike New York. Here, a man and his dog cool off in the Unisphere fountain at Flushing Meadows Corona Park.

with warm summers and cold winters.

In New York, southerly winds bring warm, humid air. These air masses collide with cold, dry air from the north. In addition, ocean air masses flow inland. This sometimes brings cool, cloudy, and damp conditions.

There is plenty of snow and rain in New York, but tornadoes are rare. Hurricanes and severe storms sometimes cause damage to Long Island, which juts into the Atlantic Ocean.

Syracuse, Rochester, Buffalo, and Binghamton are among the snowiest cities in the United States. As winter weather systems move across the Great

New Yorkers enjoy a huge snow pile. The state of New York sees plenty of snow and rain each year.

Lakes, they can pick up water. When the winds blow over land, they dump snow. The result is called lake-effect snow. New York's western region gets a lot of this kind of winter weather.

Plants and Animals

About 62 percent of New York is forested. Trees include ash, aspen, beech, birch, chestnut, cherry, dogwood, elm, hickory, pine, poplar, walnut, and willow. The state tree is the sugar maple. New York is the third-largest producer of maple syrup. About 224,000 gallons (847,932 liters) are made here every year.

The beaver is New York's state animal. In the 1600s, the rich trade in beaver pelts was one of the main reasons the Dutch and English came to this area. The city of Albany was an early trading post.

New York's other wild animals include white-tailed deer, bobcat, coyote, fox, fisher, mink, moose, muskrat, otter, raccoon, skunk, and weasel. The state has about 7,000 black bears. They mainly live in the Adirondack and Catskill Mountains.

The beaver is New York's state animal.

Deer

Otter

Mink

The bluebird is New York's state bird. Many people build nesting boxes for these songbirds. There are about 450 other species of birds in New York. They include cormorants, doves, ducks, finches, egrets, herons, geese, grebes, gulls, hawks, martins, partridge, pheasants, loons, owls, sparrows, swans, terns, woodpeckers, warblers, and bald eagles.

A cormorant looks at a New York City skyline.

About 165 fish species are in New York's inland waters. They include bass, carp, catfish, gar, herring, perch, pike, salmon, and sunfish. Brook trout is the state fish. They are mainly found in the lakes and ponds of the Adirondack Mountains, and are prized by fishermen.

A small striped bass is released back into Sandy Hook Bay off the coast of New York.

History

Giovanni da Verrazzano was the first European to visit the New York area. He was an Italian who worked for King Francis I of France. He sailed into New York Bay in 1524.

Henry Hudson followed in 1609. He sailed up the Hudson River, looking for a passage to Asia. He worked for the Dutch, who claimed the region as a colony.

The Dutch built settlements, farms, and trading posts in the area. Construction of a fort at New Amsterdam

began in 1625. The island of Manhattan was bought from a Native American tribe in 1626.

Dutch official Peter Minuit offered Native Americans trade goods in exchange for the island of Manhattan on May 24, 1626.

Nearby British settlements spilled into the Dutch areas. In 1664, three English warships made the Dutch surrender at New Amsterdam. The city and region were renamed New York.

Conflicts between the English colonies and French forces led to the French and Indian War (1754–1763). There was heavy fighting along Lake George and Lake Champlain. The French lost, and the 1763 Treaty of Paris gave the land east of the Mississippi River to England.

English soldiers fought French forces and their Native American allies near Lake George, New York, in 1755.

New York was one of the original 13 British colonies. During the American Revolution (1775-1783), the colony became a

On October 17, 1777, British General John Burgoyne surrendered to American General Horatio Gates at Saratoga, New York. The battle became a turning point toward victory for the Americans.

battleground. The British pushed back General George Washington's army and captured New York City. Many other battles were fought in New York. The American soldiers' victory at Saratoga in 1777 was a turning point in the war.

In 1783, a peace treaty was finally signed, and British forces left New York City. On July 26, 1788, New York became the 11th state to join the newly formed United States of America.

Settlers began pushing into western New York and other western territories. Better transportation was needed. The Erie Canal was completed in 1825. This waterway linked Lake Erie with the Hudson River.

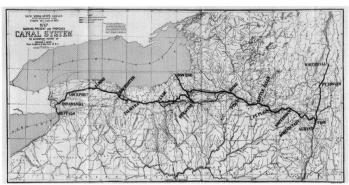

The Erie Canal allowed people and goods to be transported from New York to the Great Lakes.

The canal made it possible to ship farm products, factory goods, and immigrants from New York City into America's heartland.

Members of the 93rd New York Infantry fought in Virginia in 1863.

In the time leading up to the Civil War (1861-65), New York had strong ties to the South. But the state also had a large anti-slavery movement. When war came, about half a million New Yorkers fought for the Union North.

Following the Civil War, New York experienced huge economic growth. Many immigrants came to the state to farm or work in factories and shops.

The Great Depression started in 1929 and lasted for several years. This economic downturn hurt the state. But New York bounced back. During World War II (1939-1945), New York City's harbor was a major shipping center for the military.

Terrorists attacked New York City's World Trade Center in 1993 and 2001. The second attack destroyed the buildings, and nearly 3,000 people were killed. But New York recovered, as it has before in its history. Today, it continues to be one of the most important and powerful places in the nation and the world.

The two towers of the World Trade Center.

Twin lights glow as a memorial to the people who died on September 11, 2001.

Did You Know?

- The first European to see Niagara Falls was probably Father Louis Hennepin. He was part of a French expedition that visited the area in 1678.

- The Catskill Mountains are the home of the legendary Rip Van Winkle. In the story, Van Winkle foolishly drinks with the ghostly crew of Henry Hudson, then sleeps for 20 years. He awakens to a changed world. Author Washington Irving (1783-1859) also wrote *The Legend of Sleepy Hollow.*

- The Empire State Building was the tallest in the world when it was completed in 1931. In 1945, a U.S. Army B-25 bomber got lost in the fog and accidentally flew into the skyscraper. Fourteen people were killed and 26 injured, but the building survived.

- The Navy's USS *New York* is a transport ship that can carry about 360 sailors and 700 Marines into battle. Its bow includes 7.5 tons (6.8 metric tons) of recycled steel from the ruined World Trade Center.

People

Franklin D. Roosevelt (1882-1945) is the only United States president elected four times. He was the 32nd president, serving from 1933 to 1945. Roosevelt's plan to help the country climb out of the Great Depression was called the New Deal. He also led the United States through most of World War II. Roosevelt was born in Hyde Park.

Theodore Roosevelt

(1858-1919) was the 26th president of the United States, from 1901 to 1909. In 1898, he led the U.S. Cavalry's Rough Riders in the Spanish-American War. He served as governor of New York from 1899 to 1900. Roosevelt supported laws to break up dishonest companies. He also led the fight to conserve America's natural lands. He helped get the Panama Canal built, and won the Nobel Peace Prize in 1906. Roosevelt was born in New York City.

George Eastman (1854-1932) invented roll film, which made photography easier. It also made motion pictures possible. His Eastman Kodak Company still makes film today. Eastman was born in Waterville, New York.

Fiorello La Guardia (1882-1947) was a popular mayor of New York City from 1934 to 1945. His leadership helped New York recover from the Great Depression of the 1930s. La Guardia was born in New York City.

NEW YORK

Colin Powell (1937-) is a retired four-star general of the United States Army. He was the United States secretary of state from 2001 to 2005. He was the first African American to hold that position. Powell was born in Harlem.

Christina Aguilera (1980-) is an award-winning singer and songwriter. Her albums have sold more than 42 million copies. She was born in Staten Island, New York.

Denzel Washington (1954-) is a motion picture and television actor and director. He has won many awards, including two Academy Awards. Washington was born in Mount Vernon.

Cities

New York City is the largest city in the United States. Its population

is 8,274,527. In the early 1600s, Dutch settlers built a new fort and city on the island of Manhattan, and called it New Amsterdam. After Great Britain took over the area, the city was renamed New York. The city grew into an important port and trade center. Millions of immigrants passed through the city's port. Today, the city is a leader in trade, finance, media, art, architecture, entertainment, and fashion.

Albany has been the capital of New York since 1797. It is one of the oldest cities in the United States. The Dutch built Fort Nassau here in 1614. When Great Britain took the area in 1664, the community was renamed Albany. The state government is the city's major employer. There are also many high-technology businesses in the area. Albany's population is 94,172.

Buffalo is at the eastern end of Lake Erie. Its population is 272,632. The British burned the city during the War of 1812. The Erie Canal connected Buffalo with the Atlantic Ocean in 1825. Buffalo became a shipping and manufacturing center. Many of its industries and people left in the second half of the 20th century, but it is still New York's second-largest city. There are a several colleges in the area, including three State University of New York institutions.

Rochester grew around the Genesee River, which provided waterpower. The city manufactured flour and clothes. In modern times, the city became the home of photography giant Eastman Kodak, as well as other national companies. The University of Rochester is the largest employer. Rochester's population is 206,759.

Syracuse is in central New York. Its population is 139,079. The city is an economic, educational, and transportation center. It is a junction for the Erie Canal and railways, as well as I-81 and I-90. Syracuse University and the New York State Fair are located in the city.

Transportation

New York gained wealth and influence because of its location on major transportation routes. The harbor at New York City gave entry to America's heartland by way of the Hudson River and the Erie Canal. Later, railways and roads took their place.

Today, the combined harbors of New York and New Jersey make up the East Coast's largest port complex. In 2008, it handled about $190 billion worth of freight.

New York's railways carry more than 35 million tons (31.8 million metric tons) of freight. There is Amtrak, commuter, and subway train service.

Several busy interstate highways crisscross the state, including Interstates I-81, I-84, I-87, I-88, and I-90.

New York has 18 commercial airports. The largest are John F. Kennedy International Airport and Fiorello La Guardia Airport. JFK serves about 48 million and La Guardia serves about 23 million passengers per year.

The JFK International Airport continues to grow with a new JetBlue terminal added in 2008.

Natural Resources

New York agriculture is a $4.4 billion business. The state's 36,352 farms use about one-fifth of New York's total land area.

New York is the nation's third-largest dairy producer, and the third-largest wine and grape producer. The state ranks second in apple growing.

Empire apples are harvested in late September at a farm in Voorheesville, New York.

Other farm products include beans, cabbages, cattle, cherries, corn, maple syrup, onions, poultry, pears, and strawberries. The state is one of the largest growers of flowers and houseplants.

New York's forestry industry employs about 57,000 people. More than 1,000 farms grow Christmas trees.

New York's largest commercial fishing port is Montauk, on the eastern end of Long Island. Catches include finfish, clams, oysters, shellfish, and squid.

Sand, gravel, limestone, and gypsum, are mined in New York, as well as garnet, salt, talc, and zinc.

Lobster fishermen head out early from Montauk, Long Island. Lobster boats usually have one captain and one crewman. Much of their catch is sold to local stores. Montauk is New York's largest commercial fishing port.

Industry

New York's economy in 2007 added up to about $1.1 trillion. New York companies include leading computer, financial, imaging, media, and medical businesses.

New York City is a world center for banking and finance. The New York Stock Exchange is located here. The city is also home to giant publishing and media companies such as Time Warner and News Corporation. Major television networks based in the city include ABC, CBS, NBC, and FOX.

New York tourism is a $53 billion business. New York City is a popular place to visit, with its world-famous theaters, shopping, and landmarks. Niagara Falls is one of the best-known attractions in western New York. There are also popular resorts in the Catskill and Adirondack Mountains.

New York City is a world center for banking and finance. Thousands of people work on Wall Street.

Sports

The National Football League includes three teams from New York. They are the Buffalo Bills, the New York Giants, and the New York Jets.

The New York Mets and New York Yankees are the state's

two Major League Baseball teams.

The New York Liberty is a team in the Women's National Basketball Association. The New York Knicks, a National Basketball Association team, is in Manhattan.

The New York Rangers, New York Islanders, and

Buffalo Sabres are in the National Hockey League.

Campers and hikers enjoy New York's many parks and trails, including the famous Appalachian Trail. Water sports include boating and fishing. Hunting is popular, too.

Winter activities include dogsledding, ice fishing, and skating. New York has about 50 downhill and 50 cross-country ski areas. Lake Placid hosted the Olympic Winter Games in 1932 and 1980. It continues to host many outdoor events.

A bobsled and skeleton World Cup competition at Lake Placid.

Entertainment

New York City is famed for its cultural attractions. It often leads the nation in art, architecture, entertainment, music, photography, and theater.

Famous New York art museums include the Guggenheim Museum, Metropolitan Museum of Art, Museum of Modern Art, and the Whitney Museum of American Art.

Popular zoos are located in Central Park, Bronx, Queens, Prospect Park, and Staten Island. The cities of Buffalo and Rochester also have popular zoos. Coney Island is the state's best-known amusement park area. It is also the location of the New York Aquarium.

Car and horse racing are popular in the state. The Great New York State Fair is held at Syracuse. There are also countless festivals and fairs held throughout the state.

The unique spiral design of the Guggenheim Museum was created by the famous architect Frank Lloyd Wright. It opened in 1959.

The Metropolitan Museum of Art is one of the largest and most famous places to view both old and modern works of art.

Timeline

1609—Henry Hudson sails up the Hudson River to explore the area.

1625—Dutch settlers build a fort at New Amsterdam (New York City).

1664—British take the Dutch colony and rename it New York.

1678—Father Louis Hennepin reaches Niagara Falls.

1754–1763—French and Indian War. Important battles take place at Lake George and Lake Champlain in New York.

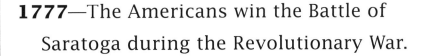

1777—The Americans win the Battle of
Saratoga during the Revolutionary War.

1788—New York becomes the 11th state.

1825—The Erie Canal is completed.

1861—Civil War begins. New York stays
in the Union.

1892—Ellis Island becomes the main
entry facility for immigrants.

1945—U.S. Army plane flies into the
Empire State Building.

2001—Terrorists attack New York City's
World Trade Center on September 11.

Glossary

Canal—A waterway that carries freight and people in boats. Canals often connect lakes and rivers.

Colony—A colony is the establishment of national or ethnic settlement in a new location. It is often ruled by another country.

Glacier—When snow gathers near the poles or on mountains, it forms a slow-moving "river of ice" called a glacier. Ice-age glaciers carved and smoothed the land underneath them.

Ice Age—A geological period of cold climate, with thick sheets of ice and snow covering the polar regions and expanding over the continents. The last major ice age peaked about 20,000 years ago.

Immigrants—People who make a foreign country their home. Many immigrants to the United States in the 1800s came to New York, or passed through the state.

Junction—A junction is a place where roads, railways, or canals meet or cross.

Lake-Effect Snow—Lake-effect snow is caused by wintertime weather systems. They pick up moisture over large bodies of water, such as Lake Erie.

Long Island Sound—A bay of water that is part of the Atlantic Ocean. The sound is between Connecticut and New York's Long Island.

Moraine—A large pile of silt and other debris left by a glacier. The deposits usually make good farmland.

Rough Riders—The 1st United States Volunteer Cavalry. When led by Theodore Roosevelt in 1898, it became one of the most famous American military fighting units in history.

Territory—An area of land controlled by a country's government. Early in its history, the United States held much territory in lands west of the established states. People settled these lands and formed communities. Eventually, the territories became states.

Index

A
ABC 38
Academy Award 29
Adirondack Mountains
   8, 14, 17, 38
Adirondack Park 8
Aguilera, Christina 29
Alaska 8
Albany, NY 14, 31
Allegheny Plateau 8
Allegheny River 10
American Revolution 20
Amtrak 34
Appalachian Mountains
   8
Appalachian Trail 41
Army, U.S. 25, 29
Asia 18
Atlantic Ocean 11, 13,
   32

B
Binghamton, NY 13
Bronx 42
Buffalo, NY 13, 32, 42
Buffalo Bills 40
Buffalo Sabres 40

C
Catskill Mountains 8,
   14, 24, 38
Cavalry, U.S. 27
CBS 38
Central Park 42
Champlain, Lake 11, 19
Civil War 22
Coney Island 42

D
Delaware River 10

E
East Coast 34
Eastman, George 28
Eastman Kodak Company
   28, 33
Empire State Building 25
England 19
Erie, Lake 10, 11, 21, 32
Erie Canal 21, 32, 33, 34

F
Finger Lakes region 11
Fort Nassau 31
FOX 38
France 18
Francis I, King of France
   18
French and Indian War 19

G
Genesee River 10, 33
George, Lake 11, 19
Great Britain 30, 31
Great Depression 22,
   26, 28
Great Lakes 13
Guggenheim Museum 42

H
Harlem 29
Hennepin, Louis 24
High Peaks region 8
Hudson, Henry 18, 24
Hudson River 10, 18,
   21, 34
Hyde Park, NY 26

I
Irving, Washington 24

J
John F. Kennedy
   International Airport
   35

L
La Guardia, Fiorello 28
La Guardia Airport 35
Lake Placid, NY 41
*Legend of Sleepy Hollow,
   The* 24
Liberty Island 4
Long Island 11, 13, 37
Long Island Sound 11

M
Major League Baseball 40
Manhattan 18, 30, 40
Marcy, Mount 8
Metropolitan Museum of
   Art 42

Mississippi River 19
Mohawk River 10
Montauk, NY 37
Mount Vernon, NY 29
Museum of Modern Art
   42

N
National Basketball
   Association 40
National Football League
   40
National Hockey League
   40
Navy, U.S. 25
NBC 38
New Amsterdam 18,
   19, 30
New Deal 26
New Jersey 34
New York, USS 25
New York Aquarium 42
New York Bay 18
New York City, NY 4, 11,
   19, 20, 21, 22, 23, 27,
   28, 30, 34, 38, 42
New York Giants 40
New York Harbor 4,
   22, 34
New York Islanders 40
New York Jets 40
New York Knicks 40
New York Liberty 40
New York Mets 40
New York Rangers 40
New York State Fair 33,
   42
New York Stock Exchange
   38
New York Yankees 40
News Corporation 38
Niagara Falls 10, 24, 38
Niagara River 10
Nobel Peace Prize 27
North 22

O
Olympic Winter Games
   41
Oneida Lake 11
Ontario, Lake 10, 11

P
Panama Canal 27
Powell, Colin 29
Prospect Park 42

Q
Queens 42

R
Rochester, NY 13, 33, 42
Roosevelt, Franklin D.
   26
Roosevelt, Theodore 27
Rough Riders 27

S
Saratoga, NY 20
Shawangunk Mountains
   8
South 22
Spanish-American War
   27
State University of New
   York 32
Staten Island, NY 29, 42
Statue of Liberty 4
Susquehanna River 10
Syracuse, NY 13, 33, 42
Syracuse University 33

T
Taconic Mountains 8
Time Warner 38
Treaty of Paris 19

U
Union 22
United States 4, 13, 21,
   26, 27, 29, 30, 31
University of Rochester
   33

V
Van Winkle, Rip 24
Verrazzano, Giovanni
   da 18

W
War of 1812 32
Washington, Denzel 29
Washington, George 20
Waterville, NY 28
Whitney Museum of
   American Art 42
Women's National
   Basketball Association
   40
World Trade Center 23,
   25
World War II 22, 26